Have you ever wondered how to deal with kids? Any adult who has dealt with a child has realized that children are very different people. Child author Jojo Yawson demystifies the child-rearing process through his insightful book, which includes ten helpful tips for dealing with kids. The delightful illustrations by child illustrator Miles Yawson truly allow adults to enter the beautiful mind of a child.

About the Author

Jojo Yawson is 8 years old and loves to read, write, and learn. He wrote this book when he was 6 years old, but he had to wait patiently for his publisher (also known as his mom's company) to publish the book.

Jojo loves swimming, fencing, playing chess, and watching YouTube history videos and TED talks.

About the Illustrator

Miles Yawson is 6 years old and loves to read, write, and learn. He illustrated this book, with the assistance of Boris Cvekić, to support his older brother Jojo's literary ambitions. In his spare time, Miles enjoys swimming, engaging in Shotokan karate, playing video games, and participating in soccer and chess matches.

How to Deal with Kids

About the Publisher

Milestales is a publishing, media, and education consulting firm that strives t
provide stories that help us grow emotionally, physically, and mentally so that we ca
achieve our greatest dreams, both individually and collectively. Milestales achieves thi
aim by producing socially conscious and culturally aware books and media. Additionall
Milestales provides training sessions, workshops, performances, arts residencies, an
enrichment programs to schools, universities, organizations, and corporations.

Milestales was founded by esteemed author, educator, and performanc
storyteller Ama Karikari-Yawson, Esq., who is also the mother of Jojo Yawson an
Miles Yawson.

Other books by Milestales

Sunne's Gift
Sunne's Gift Spanish and English Activity Book: Libro de Actividades El Don de Sunne
Earthe's Gift
All That We Need

Published by Milestales. Stories That Help Us Grow The Distance
www.milestales.com

Dear Adult,

Welcome to How to Deal with Kids!

Now you will learn the basics of how to deal with kids by reading these ten simple tips.

Thanks in advance for reading.

Love,

Jojo Yawson

Tip 1
Have Fun!

Have fun with us.

Do not bore us by taking us to the office every day.

Play with us!

Have fun by doing the things that we like with us!

Don't have so much fun that you don't do what you need to do, but have just enough fun to keep life joyful.

That is how you do it!

You did something wrong. You are not allowed to draw on the walls instead of paper. But I'm not putting you in a time out. Just don't do it again!
Ok... I understand. I won't do it again.

Tip 2
No More Timeouts

Stop giving us timeouts when we are just being kids!

Kids are kids, so don't get angry at kid behavior and don't punish us with timeouts.

Remember, you asked for this.

You asked for this when you said that you wanted children.

Don't blame us kids for just being kids.

Tip 3
Make Sure That Kids Have Time to Play with Toys

We love toys because we love to play.

Make sure that you set aside time for us to play with our toys.

But when buying toys, be selective. Too many toys are hard to clean up.

Just get the good ones.

Tip 4

Give Kids High Fives

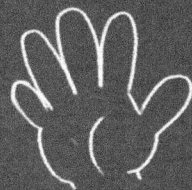

It is natural to give a high five for a good job.

Giving more high fives tells us that we are doing a good job and we are the best.

Tip 5
Give Kids Money and Robots

Give us money and robots for birthdays and holidays.

Robots are fun, and you want us to have fun. (Please see Tip 1).

Money is also a great gift because money is important, and you want us to be financially secure when we grow up.

12

Tip 6
Take Kids to Fun Places

Take us to fun places as much as you can.

There are plenty of fun places like parks, historical landmarks, children's museums, amusement parks, and game places.

Many of these places are more fun than home, so get out the house from time to time and take us to fun places in our neighborhoods, around the country, and around the world.

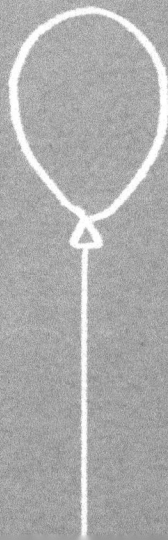

Tip 7

Read Books to Kids

We love being read to because books are great.

Do you remember being a kid and having a
favorite book or book series?

We will probably love that book or book series
too. So read those books to us.

The princess died. But when the knight gave her a kiss, she came back to life, and they lived happily ever after.
The End

16

Tip 8
Get Down to Our Level

Get down to our level when you are speaking to us.

You are probably between five feet and seven feet tall.

We are probably under four feet tall.

You are a giant to us!

We are like mice to you!

Get down to our level when you speak so you won't be so scary to us.

17

Tip 9
No Lectures

We hate lectures. We kids are often thinking about video games when adults are lecturing us.

Have conversations with us instead of lecturing us so that we can feel that our voices are also important.

We kids have thoughts and feelings too.

19

Tip 10
Fill Our Hearts with ♡
Love

Yes, fill our hearts with love by surrounding us with love.

Tell us that you love us.

Show us that you love us.

Write us love notes.

Show love to everyone around us so that our hearts can be filled with love from every angle.

We need love.

Conclusion Letter ✏️

Dear Adult,

Now you have learned how to deal with kids.

Thanks for reading.

Love,

Jojo Yawson

milestales

stories that help us grow the distance

Certificate of Completion

THIS ACKNOWLEDGES THAT

_____

HAS LEARNED THE BASICS
OF HOW TO DEAL WITH KIDS.

Signed:_____

Dated:_____

www.ingramcontent.com/pod-product-compliance
Lightning Source LLC
Chambersburg PA
CBHW060754150426

42811CB00058B/1405